eCLEANmagazine™

Issue 51

Handling Negative Reviews Positively

Featuring:

- Gerard Petersen's Story: 200+ Fake 1-Star Reviews in 10 Minutes:
- Do's and Don'ts of Negative Reviews

...and more!

1.800.433.2113

SUPPLIES   CHEMICALS   TRAINING

PROWLER

- Electric start engine
- Optional wheel kit
- Hour meter
- Oil sight glass on pump
- Belt drive pump with optional clutch
- Steel belt guard
- Quick couple plumbing connections
- Shock absorbing engine base
- Downstream chemical injection
- Schedule 80 steel heating coils
- Pressure gauge
- Pressure relief valve
- 4 color coded, quick coupled nozzles

- Optional clutch drive
- Optional honda engine
- Optional wheel kit
- Optional stainless steel frame

Model	DP-4030D	DP-5535D	DP-5540D	DP-8030D	DP-8035D	DP-1025D
PSI:	3,000	3,500	4,000	3,000	3,500	2,500
GPM:	4	5.5	5.5	8	8	10
Motor Make:	Vanguard	Vanguard	Vanguard	Vanguard	Vanguard	Vanguard
HP:	13	16	16	23	23	23
Pump Make:	DELUX® TSS1511	DELUX® TSS1811	DELUX® TSS1811	DELUX® TSF2021	DELUX® TSF2021	DELUX® TSF2221

Clearly Clean™ XTREME Concrete Cleaner

Top Rated ★★★★★

"We used it to clean a really nasty area. I have one thing to say... WOW! This cleaner not only kicks grease in the butt, it will also give you an edge over the other guy. We only use this now for all my commercial cleaning."

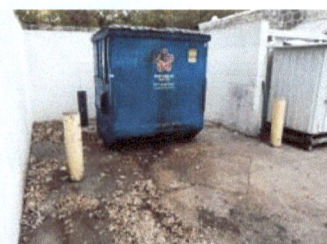

- Use this crystal clear concrete cleaner in sensitive areas where colored chemicals might draw unwanted attention
- Penetrate dirt, and lift out heavy oil stains
- Sold as a highly concentrated powder so it can be strong enough for any job

www.eCleanMag.com Issue 51

In This Issue:

4

4	200+ Fake Negative Reviews in Less Than 10 Minutes: Gerard Petersen's Story
12	Do's and Don'ts of Negative Reviews, by Allison Hester, Publisher, and Matt Adwell, Adwell Services
22	New Study Finds Use of Cleaning Chemicals as Dangerous to Lungs as Smoking a Pack a Day
24	Industry Event Calendar
26	Understanding Respiratory Protective Equipment, by Linda Chambers, Soap Warehouse/GCE
32	Announcing PowerClean 2018: CETA & PWNA, October 19-21, Orlando, Florida
33	The Principles for Setting Hour Rates, by Tom Grandy, Grandy & Associates

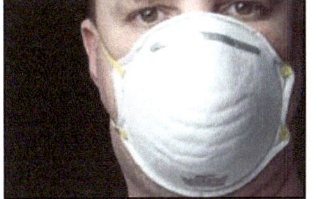

26

Cover photo courtesy of Gerard Petersen, Petersen Pressure Wash, www.PetersenPressureWash.com

eClean Magazine
Publisher/Editor: Allison Hester, allison@ecleanmag.com
    eClean Magazine
    8305 Pennwood Dr.
    Sherwood, AR 72120
    (501) 517-1620

Long Lasting, Easy to Apply, and a Breeze to Maintain

Armstrong-Clark Wood Stains condition wood beautifully

No stripping or sanding required for maintenance coats

Natural oil-based formula

Can be applied in direct sunlight and the heat of the day

No peeling, cracking, or sticky shiners

Can be exposed to rain 60 minutes after absorption into wood

One or two coats; second coat can be applied wet-on-wet

Footprints during application blend in during curing

Backed by six generations of experience in the field of wood preservation.

Armstrong-Clark stain provides two layers of protection with a single brush stroke. Drying oils stay at the surface creating a barrier that is dry to the touch. This locks in and protects the non-drying oils that penetrate deep into the wood fibers to condition and rejuvenate the wood.

Armstrong-Clark's oil based wood stains are top rated by the wood restoration website DeckStainHelp.com, including our #1 rated Mahogany and Amber colors for exotic hardwoods like Ipe and Teak.

Contact us to find an authorized dealer

Includes water repellents, mildewcide, UV inhibitors

VOC compliant in all 50 states

Long Lasting, Easy to Apply, and a Breeze to Maintain

www.armclark.com
800-565-8211

200+ Fake One-Star Reviews in 10 Minutes

by Allison Hester, Publisher

On January 14, Gerard Petersen and his wife were getting ready for bed when his phone dinged.

Looking to see what the notification was about, he realized someone had left a one-star review on Facebook for his company, Petersen Pressure Wash in West Berlin, NJ. "I wonder what that's about."

Then his phone dinged again.
And again.
And again.

"Every time I refreshed my phone, there were more notifications. More one-star reviews."

In fact, he was so surprised, he started posting about it on Facebook as it was happening.

"Apparently my Facebook has been hacked with over 100 1-star reviews!! Going to try to get in touch with Facebook ASAP!"

And a few moments later…

"Over 150 1 Star reviews in 6 minutes? Come on now."

The incident didn't last long.

Within about 10 minutes, Gerard received 218 one-star reviews on his Facebook business page. No comments. Just one star.

"At first glance, I thought, 'Oh my gosh. I'm getting all these bad reviews!' But then in looking more closely at the profiles of the people leaving the ratings, I realized they were all coming from out of the country. India. Bangladesh. There was one from France. Obviously not in the U.S., and I've never pressure washed in any of those areas ...at least not yet!"

The next day, Gerard began researching similar incidents and learned that people can actually purchase both fake positive or negative ratings from companies – particularly overseas – for an extremely low price. However, while it's easy for people to purchase fake ratings, it's a lot harder to get

88% Of Consumers Trust Online Reviews As Much As Personal Recommendations.

88%

Infographics in this article provided by Invesp, www.invespcro.com/blog/the-importance-of-online-customer-reviews-infographic/

those ratings removed.

In fact, Facebook's policy states: "You can only report star ratings that include reviews." And none of the 217 fake ratings included "reviews," i.e., comments. And just FYI: this is a common policy among other sites that allow ratings, including Google.

Gerard also quickly realized that there really is no easy way to "get in touch with Facebook" – right away" or otherwise. Facebook has no customer service line that you can call. There is not option for talking to a live person. And you can only file a complaint for ratings that go against their policies, and their policy says they'll only consider removing one-star ratings that also have a review.

Instead, Gerard had to find another way to deal with the situation.

First he continued posting on Facebook and keeping his customers and potential customers updated on the situation.

THE IMPORTANCE OF ONLINE CUSTOMER REVIEWS

90% of consumers read online reviews before visiting a business.

Customers are likely to spend 31% more on a business with "excellent" reviews.

72% say that positive reviews make them trust a local business more.

86% of people will hesitate to purchase from a business that has negative online reviews.

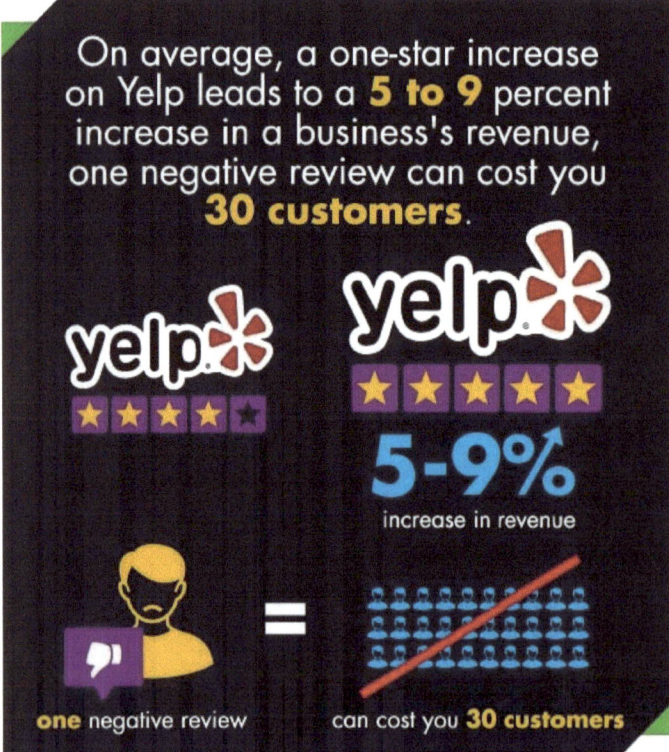

Second, he hired a lawyer.

Third, he offered a $500 reward to anyone who could provide proof of the person responsible for the fraudulent attack.

And finally, he contacted a local TV news station.

On January 18, Gerard was featured on the evening news (Fox 29) in a heartfelt interview about what had happened to him. As he told the reporter his story, he also explained: "I'm scared because as the father of five – three of my own and my two stepsons – this is how

I support my family. This is how I feed my kids and I'm scared it's going to impact my business."

Gerard immediately began getting positive responses from the news story. "The minute the story aired, people started liking my Facebook page. People started messaging me. People shared the story. People contacted to let me know they were going to support me. It was a miracle. My phone – which had completely stopped ringing after the fake reviews showed up – started ringing again. I began scheduling jobs and doing estimates."

And the media's help did not stop there. Another local station, Action News, also contacted Gerard for a story that will run sometime in April or May. "Action News also advised me they were going to be in constant contact with Facebook."

Somehow – apparently with the help of Action News as well as another organization called DTopp – the fake reviews

disappeared completely by February 10, just shy of four weeks after they first appeared.

Gerard's Advice

While Gerard's situation was a bit extreme, it could have happened to anyone. Through his experience, Gerard shared the following advice:

1. Modify the "Country Restrictions" on your Facebook business page. To do this, click on "settings," then look for the "Country Restrictions" (it was the ninth option down on my page when I wrote this) and change it to only include the country where you reside. This will prevent people who are obviously out of your service area from being able to access your page.

2. Get along with your competition as best you can. "We get to know our competition more because of social media, and there are a lot of strong personalities online," Gerard explained. "That said, it really is important to try to get along with others in your area for your own benefit."

3. If you feel it's warranted, turn to professionals for help. As mentioned earlier, Gerard did hire a lawyer, although the person(s) involved has not been identified with certainty. He also turned to a professional company called DTopp that helps get negative/false reviews removed.

4. Contact the media. For Gerard, this was the key factor that turned a bad situation into something positive.

"I imagine whoever instigated the fake reviews is now kicking himself," Gerard concluded. "In the long run, it actually helped me get good, honest publicity.

ENVIROSPEC.COM

Clean **faster, better, safer** with *Foam* **instead of pressure!**

Fat Daddy
Complete Soft-Wash System

Throw *Fat Foam* or other cleaning chemicals as high as 50 feet straight up!

The key is high-volume pumping. Watch as this speedy soft-wash system does most of the work *for* you!

Thick, foaming soft-wash detergents dwell on the surface, instead of bouncing off like regular detergents under high-pressure. That means you'll *spend less money on chemicals.* And since you can cover such large areas from one spot, *the job will take less time.*

High pressure is great for things like concrete, but what happens when you use it on roof shingles? It dislodges the granules, damaging the customer's roof. Siding and other surfaces can also suffer under high pressure. The high-performance *Fat Daddy soft-wash system is the state-of-the-art answer* for today's cleaning pro's.

You'll have everything you need to get the job done right. It's the quick-cleaning system for roofs, siding *and* trucks!

This is one powerful, durable package, engineered around *intelligent design.*
• Fat Daddy 3-cylinder *high-volume pump, custom designed for soft-wash cleaning,* and made to handle the harshest chemicals
• Rugged yet quiet 7.0 horsepower *quick-starting Kohler engine*
• Fat Daddy Long Distance Foam Turbine, and high-impact Predator nozzle, plus lance assembly and discharge hose
• Additional accessories included, so you can get right to work

Check out the details, videos and prices at:
Envirospec.com/fatdaddy

Find out why professionals who try EnviroSpec equipment and chemicals stop using everything else.

FIGHT DIRTY

19HP GAS HOT WATER PRESSURE WASHER TRAILER

- Kohler EFI 694cc engine
- 5.5 GPM; 4000 PSI
- 400-gal. water tank
- 2-24-gal. chemical tanks
- 7200-lb. tandem axel trailer

#157563

$18,999.99

FREE SHIPPING!

TESTED ★ TOUGH
25,000 HOURS + 25,000 MILES OF COMBINED TESTING

EXCLUSIVE NORTHSTAR PROSHOT TECHNOLOGIES

 Heat Storm downdraft heat exchanger provides up to 35% increased fuel efficiency over traditional updraft burners.

 Prime Plus flooded pump inlet improves priming and extends pump life by positioning the pump below the fluid level.

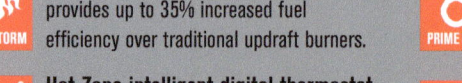 **Hot Zone intelligent digital thermostat** delivers accurate temperature regulation with 15–18°F accuracy.

 Water Sense low water shutdown protects pump from running dry, automatically shutting off engine when water tank is empty.

 Heat Boost provides industry-leading 150°F temperature rise, guaranteeing a minimum of 182°F for maximum cleaning efficiency.

PRICES START AT $7999.99 — PICK YOUR PROSHOT PRESSURE WASHER

13HP Gas Skid
FREE SHIPPING! #157560

19HP Gas Skid + Tank
FREE SHIPPING! #157573

21HP Diesel Trailer
FREE SHIPPING! #157569

More models available. Call 1-800-969-7073 Ext. 22 for information. Keycode 259637

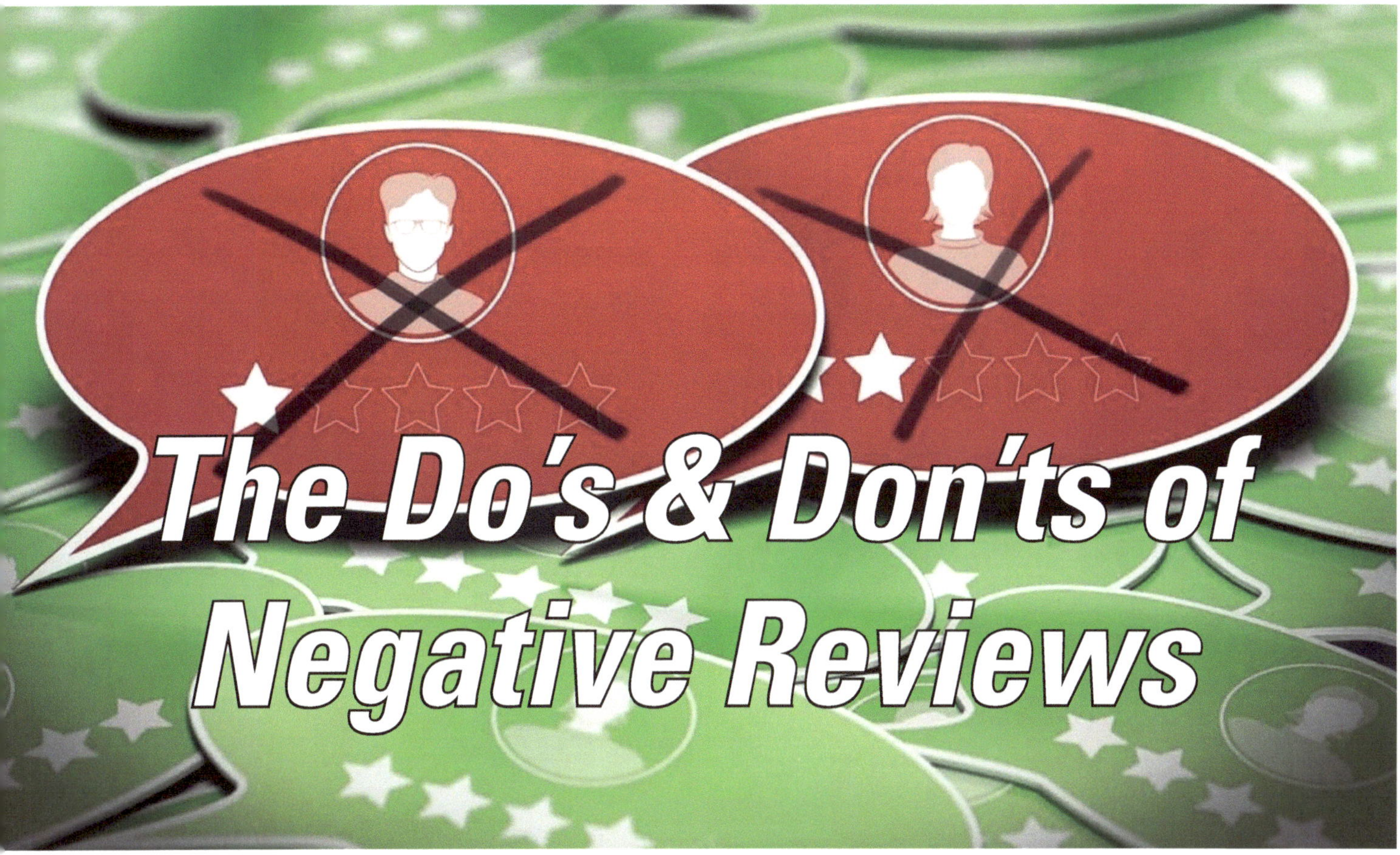

The Do's & Don'ts of Negative Reviews

by Allison Hester, Publisher & Matt Adwell, Adwell Services

Publisher's Note: For this article, I turned not only Internet research, but I also called on Matt Adwell of Adwell Services to help customize the content after seeing how he brilliantly handled a negative online review from a former employee.

This issue's cover story told about one contractor's nightmare of receiving over 200 fake one-star reviews within about a 10 minute time frame. While that situation was (hopefully) unusual, getting a bad review from time to time *can* happen, and it's important to know how to respond.

The Positives of Negatives

1. If you get a negative review or two, don't panic. In some ways this may actually be a good thing.

In fact, studies are finding that people don't necessarily trust companies or products that have only five star ratings. When customers see nothing but glowing reviews, they often begin to question their legitimacy. Are these positive reviews fake? Are they censoring negative reviews? Are they offering incentives for positive reviews? Are they only

In fact, studies are finding that people don't necessarily trust companies or products that have only five stars. When customers see nothing but glowing reviews, they often begin to question their legitimacy.

getting reviews from friends and family? And so on. By having a couple of negative reviews visible, people see that your company has nothing to hide, which can be good for you in the long run.

2. If you get a negative review, remember that it doesn't necessarily mean your service was bad. Most likely, the negative review resulted from unmet expectations on the part of the reviewer.

A Yotpo study of 1.3 million reviews found that the most commonly used negative words in reviews – which were mentioned 20,000 times – were "disappointment" or "disappointed." In fact, the next common negative word – i.e., "bad" – was only mentioned 7,500 times.

Disappointments occur when expectations aren't met. So figuring out what's really important to your customers – e.g., "Don't trample Aunt Martha's rose bushes" – as well as helping them understand what they should and should not expect from you before you clean can go a long way in avoiding unmet expectations.

3. When you have a couple of negative reviews, your positive reviews shine brighter. If the vast majority of your reviews are four or five stars, and then there's a stray one or two star stuck in there, people are going to naturally think that whoever wrote the negative review is probably just a crotchety old grump.

4. By responding positively to your negative reviews, there are times that you can show your business in a more favorable light that you could have without the negative review. I've heard many stories from contractors who were able to turn their mistakes into positives and create raving fans, all because of the way they handled the situation one on one with their clients. That same principle can help you understand how to deal with negative online reviews.

Don'ts and Do's for Responding to Negative Reviews

First, the don'ts:

1. Don't ignore the elephant: Whether the review is warranted or not, it's there, on your permanent record. Wishing it would just disappear doesn't work. Ignoring the review gives the impression that you don't care about what your clients (or potential clients) think, and that could be worse than the review itself.

2. Don't procrastinate: If someone goes to the trouble of complaining online about your service, make sure you go to the trouble of responding, and do so promptly. That being said, if you need to wait because you are too angry to respond, *do it*. Waiting to cool off before going on a typing rampage is crucial.

3. Don't argue or get defensive: This one can be hard, especially if you are in the right, or worse, the review is fake. (We'll talk more about fake reviews in a moment.) Arguing makes you look worse,

like you can't take criticism, and can spiral out of control quickly.

Now for the Do's:

1. Remember who you're talking to: Yes, you are responding to an unhappy customer. However, you are doing so in front of every potential customer who reads your response. How do you want them to see you? As a reasonable person whom they would want to work with? As a person who blames others when things don't go your way? You can't control the review, but you can control the perception of your company.

2. Carefully think out your response: A knee-jerk response is not the right way to go, but neither is a canned response. Unhappy customers want to feel like they've been heard, and a canned response does not provide that sense of validity. In fact, one article said that 33 percent of negative reviews on Yelp turned positive when someone took the time to respond to their review.

3. Apologize if appropriate: Apologies disarm the complainant. Did you drop the ball? Acknowledge it. Did you make a mistake? Own it.

Everyone makes mistakes. Apologize, then tell what measures you've taken to prevent this problem in the future. Explain that this is not the normal experience with your service. Offer to not charge for the work. Take responsibility! Most folks will find this refreshing. Plus, it tells potential customers that you run toward problems, take them seriously, and work to fix them, which can be more important than telling how great you are if everything goes right.

4. Clearly identify the problem: Take your emotion about getting a negative review out the equation. What is the person *really* upset about? Some complaints are solely about cost or something else that has nothing to do with the quality of your service.

In a recent review, a client complained about the cost while acknowledging that the work and service received were top notch. Personally, I'd ignore the complaint about the money and

focus on the fact that we take pride in our quality work and customer service.

5. Take the Conversation Offline: "Please call or email me at (contact information) to discuss how I can resolve this to your satisfaction." This allows you to deal with the situation in a private manner, plus makes it easy for others who are impressed by your professional manner of handling the situation to contact␣your as well. If the customer continues to respond negatively, you can again ask them to contact you personally, then drop it. Continuing to engage with someone wanting to pick a fight online does not reflect well.

Along these same lines, if you get a negative review and don't really understand why, you may want to contact that customer to find out what you could have done differently. I recently spoke with a contractor who had just gotten his only one-star review, but the words the lady posted were all positive. After messaging to see what he could have done differently, the customer realized she mistakenly put one star and changed the review.

> **Let's get real. It is not at all unheard of for competitors, disgruntled employees, etc., to make up fake negative reviews. Then what can you do?**

6. Respond to positive reviews as well. Again, if someone takes the time to post a review, let them know you appreciate it – even if it's a simple "thank you" or even a press of the "like" button.

Dealing with Fake Reviews

OK, all of the above is well and good when dealing with legitimate dissatisfied customers. However, let's get real. It is not at all unheard of for competitors, disgruntled employees, etc., to make up fake negative reviews. Then what can you do?

This is when you report a review with the host site (e.g., Facebook, Yelp, etc). However, you need to read the site's rules for what they consider to be reportable reviews.

For example, Facebook will potentially remove reviews that "don't follow the Facebook community standards or don't focus on the product or service offered by the Page." However, "you can only report star ratings that include reviews." So if you get one star with no verbiage to explain why, they generally won't consider removing it.

Yelp says they will consider removing a negative review "if it's clear that it was posted by someone with a conflict of interest, including reviews from current or former employees, competitors or peers, or friends and family members of the business owner – even if they insist they were actually a customer and were uninfluenced by their relation to the business." However, Yelp goes on to add the following: "Please note that it usually isn't enough to say that you're suspicious of a bias. It must be clear to our moderators that there's a conflict of interest, so please provide specific evidence when you report the review."

JIM DUBOIS' WINDOW WASHING WEALTH SYSTEM!

If You're One of the THOUSANDS of Window Washers Across the U.S. ...
"I'll personally help you build a six-figure, cash-generating, window washing empire like mine. Yes, I'll work with you."

My name is Jim DuBois, and today I run a strong, automated, six-figure income, systemized window cleaning empire. I've been using my easy-to-implement system to make $250,000+ a year, year after year.

And the fact is, anyone can copy my success once they have the right tools, and my personal help.

I know how to quickly go from no clients to $250,000 in automatic income without making all the typical mistakes. I'll save you a ton of time and money and show you how to:

✔ Build your business with minimal expense.
✔ Make more money fast ... Not months or years, but days. Even if you're part-time.
✔ Earn a strong, six-figure income and join the top 1% of elite window cleaning earners.
✔ Develop a lifestyle where you work when you want, and the money STILL keeps coming in.
✔ Implement my extremely effective marketing strategies to create wealth, from attracting the right employees, to ultimately eliminating your competition.

I'll give you EVERY tool you need to succeed.

It's My Proven System. BUT ... The most valuable part of my system is my personal, 1-on-1 help that guides you every step of the way and it starts with a Free Report.

I FOCUS ON 2 PRIMARY MARKETS:
1. **Commercial (Storefronts, Chains, Shopping Centers, and Malls)**
2. **Residential (Homes, Townhomes, Condos, and Apartments)**

I know this business inside and out, and have made my living for over 20 years. I'm still learning new, better ways to grow our business.

And ... It won't take you 5, 10, or 20 years to reach a 6-figure income level. I can show you how to make $150,000 to $300,000 a year within just two to three years. Guaranteed.

I can show you how to strategically build your business. And all you need is the willingness to follow my lead. I will take you by the hand on a day-to-day basis, and work with you until your income is substantial. You WILL get there.

Now, does everyone make this kind of money? No, of course not. Those in the window cleaning business know it's not hard to make a decent living of $40,000 or $50,000 a year. But very few know the right approach, the secrets and strategies to make the big money by learning how to dominate and monopolize their marketplace.

AND THAT'S WHAT I DO BEST!
But, that's NOT what everyone wants to do. Some are happy to simply take my knowledge and double their income to $80,000 or $90,000. But I can help you get more ...

Not just more money. But also a lifestyle others are envious of. Who really wants to wash windows 5 or 6 days a week, for 10 hours a day? Not many people I know.

Call right now for your FREE No Risk – No Obligation Consultation. Once you hear what I have to share, and you see how much help I can give to get your business to the next level, and way beyond, you'll be excited, wanting to know more. To learn more... go to WindowWashingWealth.com for your FREE Report

Call Now 704-799-0313
for a FREE CONSULTATION
Go to WindowWashingWealth.com
for Your FREE REPORT

CALL NOW FOR A FREE CONSULTATION & REPORT: 704-799-0313 ext 2

What can be considered evidence – especially if the reviewer uses a false name? Here are some things to watch for:

1. **Cleaning industry lingo heavy.** Most customers aren't going to know some of the unique terms used by the industry, but competitors or employees likely will. Their natural inclination is to throw in some of those terms when writing a review.

2. **Weak profiles.** Depending on the site – such as on Facebook – you can look at the profile of the reviewer. If the person has little to no activity history, the account is likely fake.

3. **Similar lingo on other competitors' sites.** Look for similar reviews from the same person (or at least using the same language) on your competitors' sites. If it is a competitor, they may be attacking more than just your company. You might also look at your competitor's site to see if that same profile that left a bad review on your site left a glowing review on one of your competitors' pages.

4. **You have no record of the person in your customer files.** This may help in the reporting process, but it may not, as most review sites don't require the reviewer to actually be a customer.

5, **Reviewer is not open to talking with you offline.** As mentioned earlier, you want to try to remedy problems offline. If you offer that opportunity and either don't hear from the "customer" or they continue to argue online but refuse to contact you offline, document this for when you flag the review.

6. **Words don't match what you offer.** A common sign of malicious reviews is that the products, services, or facilities don't line up with what your business actually entails.

> **Even if the fake review is not removed, there are things that can be done to reduce any negative impact.**

Once you gather evidence, you can flag the fake negative reviews on the site, including the details you've found (such as screenshots, internal documentation, etc.) to back up your claim. Be sure you check several review sites. This will increase your chances of getting the fake review removed, and potentially speed up the process as well.

At this point, your fate is largely in the hands of the review site. However, there are services out there that can help you get fake negative reviews removed from your website, and they often don't charge unless they are successful.

Even if the fake review is not removed, there are things that can be done to reduce any negative impact:

1. Call them out subtly: If the person has never been a client of your company, explain that you provide great customer service, but unfortunately this person is not a client of your business. If it is a former employee, address that head on. Most people quickly dismiss reviews from fake clients and bitter former employees.

2. Drown them in positivity: If you provide great service and have the habit of collecting good reviews from happy clients, a fake negative review will stand out like a sore thumb and will seem less credible.

3. Stay classy: Regardless of how low some people go, do not stoop to their level. Your determination to remain classy in the face of negativity will play well with potential clients.

A Quick Final Note

As business owners, you understand the value of positive reviews. As such, I'd like to encourage you to keep that in mind as you deal with other businesses daily. People tend to tell everyone about bad experiences and keep good experiences to themselves. So if you have a positive experience – whether it's buying a $20,000 vehicle, or a $2 hamburger – be sure to let that business know, preferably online where it can be seen by others.

About the Author

Matt Adwell is president of Adwell Services, a residential and commercial maintenance company in Annapolis, MD. Matt has been cleaning professionally for 25 years. To learn more, visit www.AdwellServices.com.

WATER FED
GUTTERS
HOMES
AWNINGS
LADDER SAFETY
SYSTEMIZE OSHA
PRESSURE WASH
CONCRETE
HARD WATER
SOFT WASH
MARKETING

Sign Up Today!
jracenstein.com/events/

CHISEL

with 'high-yield' Gloss Enhancers

VOTED THE INDUSTRY'S HOTTEST NEW TRUCK WASH!

Chisel is a professional strength alkaline detergent that has been formulated to be the industry's most effective 'super-duty' truck wash for neglected, oxidized and 'hard to clean' commercial vehicles.

Special rinse agents make the detergent 'sheet' off the surface to shorten rinsing time. Loaded with extra 'gloss enhancers', Chisel is sure to make your job a lot easier and your customer a lot happier.

This product can be used as a single step cleaner or as step #2 in a 'two-step' cleaning application. Chisel has been pH balanced to be an outstanding second step of "Twin Chem" cleaning. For the absolute very best results, downstream inject using the industry's highest drawing and #1 selling chemical injector - the Allison Super Suds Sucker - our part number 1964

Packaging: One 60-pound carton of powder with 8 pounds of super solvent additive will yield 55 gallons of liquid detergent concentrate and a double dose of gloss enhancers.

Go to **EnviroSpec.com** and Search for Part No. **CH55**

New Study Finds Use of Cleaning Chemicals as Damaging to Lungs as Smoking a Pack a Day

by Allison Hester, Publisher

In mid-February, the University of Bergen in Norway released its findings from a 20-year scientific study on the impact of cleaning chemicals on lung function. The study determined that the regular use of cleaning sprays containing chemicals such as bleach, hydrogen peroxide, and ammonia can cause as much damage to lung function as smoking 20 cigarettes per day.

The study followed over 6,000 participants – 3,298 women and 2,932 men – who were separated into three categories: those who were occupational cleaners, those who used cleaning products at least once a week in their homes, and those who rarely used cleaning products. The participants' lung function was measured by the amount of air they could forcefully breathe out after breathing in. The study also controlled variables that could affect lung capacity, such as smoking.

In the end, occupational cleaners showed the highest amount of lung damage – including asthma. However, even those participants who used cleaning sprays to clean their homes at least once per week showed a marked increase of damage in their lung function compared to those who did not.

The study found that women were impacted more than men, but scientists also claimed that the discrepancy may have been due to the smaller number of men who participated.

The Norway study's findings were similar to those of a September 2017 study in France that followed over 55,000 registered nurses for over eight years with no prior history of chronic obstructive pulmonary disease (COPD). The French study found that nurses who used disinfectants at least once a week to clean surfaces showed a 24 to 32 percent increased risk of developing COPD compared to those who did not.

The research adds to previously reported concerns about the presence of volatile organic compounds (VOCs) in cleaning products. These types of chemicals evaporate into the air when they are used, including acetone, benzene and formaldehyde. Best advice is to avoid breathing in too many VOCs on a regular basis.

Experts attribute the decline in lung function to the damage cleaning agents cause to mucous membranes lining the airways, resulting in persistent changes over time.

Co-author Oistein Svanes said: "The take-home message is that in the long run cleaning chemicals very likely cause rather substantial damage to your lungs. These chemicals are usually unnecessary; microfiber cloths and water are more than enough for most purposes."

Industry Events

April

April 25-28: International Kitchen Exhaust Cleaning Association (IKECA) Annual Membership Meeting, San Diego, CA, www.IKECA.org

April 26-28: The Experience Conference & Exhibition, Atlanta, GA, www.experiencetheevents.com

May

May 4-5: Power Wash Store Open House, Nashville, TN, www.PowerWashStore.com

August

August 23-24: The Huge Convention, Atlanta, GA, www.TheHugeConvention.com

September

Sept. 5-7: The Experience Convention & Trade Show, Las Vegas, NV www.experiencetheevents.com

October

October 3-6: International Kitchen Exhaust Cleaning Association (IKECA) Technical Seminar and Expo, Indianapolis, IN, www.IKECA.org

October 18-21: PWNA/CETA National Convention, Orlando, FL, www.PWNA.org

Oct. 29 - Nov. 1: International Sanitary Supply Association (ISSA) Interclean, Dallas, TX www.ISSA.com

November

Nov. 2-3: Southside Equipment Education and Networking Event, Brooks, KY, www.pressurewasherky.us

January

Jan. 22-25 World of Concrete, Las Vegas, NV, www.WorldofConcrete.com

January 25-27: International Cleaning Expo (ICE), Las Vegas, NV, www.ICEexpo.org

February

Feb. 11-14: International Window Cleaning Association (IWCA) Annual Convention & Trade Show, San Diego, CA, www.IWCA.org

March

March. 6-8: Painting and Decorating Contractors of America (PDCA) Painting Contractors Expo, Savannah, GA, www.PDCA.org

March. 26-27: Clean Buildings Expo (CBE), Baltimore, MD, www.ISSA.com

November

Nov. 18-21: International Sanitary Supply Association (ISSA) North America, Las Vegas, NV, www.ISSA.com

For a more comprehensive list of events, visit www.eCleanMag.com/Events

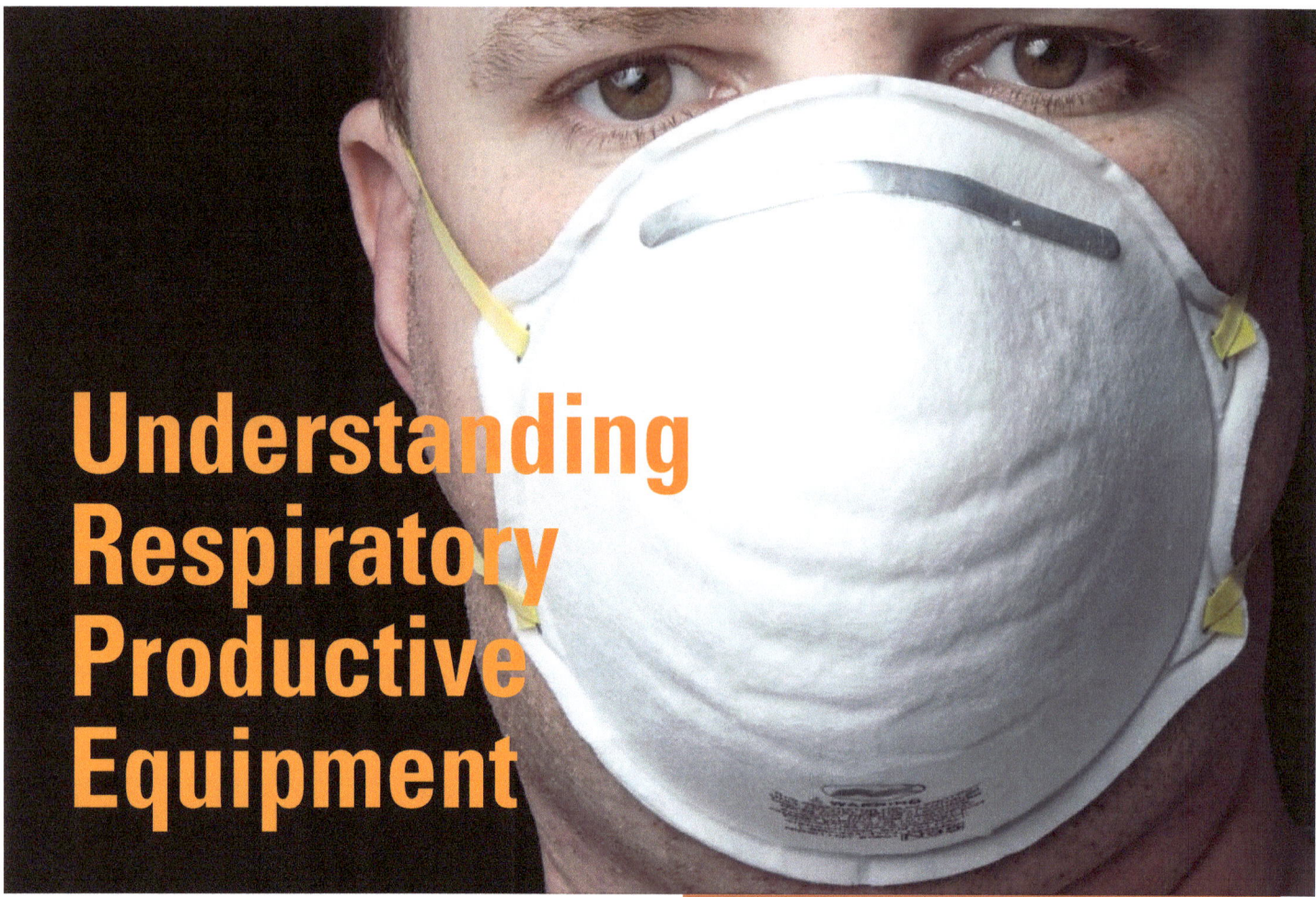

Understanding Respiratory Productive Equipment

by Linda Chambers, Soap Warehouse/GCE

Respiratory Protective Equipment (RPE) is a particular type of personal protective equipment (PPE) and is one of the most important. Too frequently, however, it is also one of the first to be misused or not used at all.

But not wearing PPE is only part of the issue. Employees often try to be protected but use the incorrect type of PPE for the job they are doing or are don't take other protective measures that should have been done as well.

For instance: 66% of injured workers were wearing safety shoes,

Contract labor workers have been shown to most likely wear PPE in this order:

1. Protective footwear
2. Hard hat
3. Glasses or protective eyewear
4. Gloves
5. Dust mask
6. Safety Harness
7. Ear plugs
8. Respirator

protective footwear, heavy-duty shoes or boots, while 33% had on regular street shoes. Of those wearing safety shoes, 85% were injured because the object hit an unprotected part of the shoe or boot or they were performing the work unsafely for the boots to help.

But let us get back to our topic today, RPE.

There are a few different levels to what RPE is needed and what a particular respirator can do for the wearer. You first need to know what one is and what it's limitations are.

A respirator is a device that protects you from inhaling dangerous substances, such as chemicals and infectious particles. Selecting the right respirator requires an assessment of all the workplace operations, processes or environments that may create a respiratory hazard. The identity of the hazard and its airborne concentrations need

to be determined before choosing a respirator.

Respirators work by either filtering particles from the air, chemically cleaning (purifying) the air, or supplying clean air from an outside source.

There are several different types of respirators, as described below.

Particulate Respirators:

Particulate respirators are the simplest, least expensive, and least protective of the respirator types available. These respirators only protect against particles (dust). They do not protect against chemicals, gases, or vapors, and are intended only for low hazard levels.

The commonly known "N-95" filtering respirator or "dust mask" (below) is one type of particulate respirator, often used in hospitals to protect against infectious agents. Particulate respirators are "air purifying respirators" because they clean particles out of the air as you breathe.

Contractors have a misconception that N-95 will protect them when applying chemicals while cleaning and that is completely wrong.

Here are some facts from OSHA and data from the Bureau of Labor Statistics from 1980.

- **Hard hats were worn by only 16% of those workers who sustained head injuries, although two-fifths were required to wear them for certain tasks at specific locations;**

- **Only 1% of approximately 770 workers suffering face injuries were wearing face protection;**

- **Only 23% of the workers with foot injuries wore safety shoes or boots; and**

- **About 40% of the workers with eye injuries wore eye protective equipment.**

Particulate respirators:
- Filter out dusts.
- Are usually disposable masks or respirators with disposable filters.
- Must be replaced when they become discolored, damaged, or clogged.

Chemical Cartridge/Gas Mask Respirator

Gas masks are also known as "air-purifying respirators" because they filter or clean chemical gases out of the air as you breathe. This type of respirator includes a face piece or mask, and a cartridge or canister. Straps secure the mask to the head to secure over the face (mouth and nose). The cartridge may also have a filter to remove particles to be duel purpose.

Gas masks are effective only if used with the correct cartridge or filter for a particular chemical or biological substance. Selecting the proper filter can be complicated. Cartridges are available that protect against more than one hazard, but there is no "all-in-one" cartridge that protects against all substances. It is important to know what hazards you will face in order to be certain you are choosing the right filters/cartridges.

- Uses replaceable chemical cartridges or canisters to remove the contaminant.
- Are color-coded to help you select the right one.
- May require more than one cartridge to protect against multiple hazards.

The gas mask is the one most cleaning contractors should be using in their daily work. Paying careful attention to the type of filter needed and hours used for replacement.

The highest reason for failure of a gas mask right after improper fit is expired or exhausted life of the filter itself.

The next step above the normal gas mask is the *Powered Air-Purifying Respirator (PAPR)*.

Powered air-purifying respirators use a fan to draw air through the filter to the user. They are easier to breathe

through, since the person's own lungs are not used to pull air through the mask; however, they need a fully-charged battery to work properly. They use the same type of filters/cartridges as other air-purifying respirators. It is important to know what the hazard is, and how much of it is in the air, in order to select the proper filters/cartridges. Also using these can shorten the life span of the filter itself since the pull through the filter is constant with the fan versus the person's own in-and-out breathing.

There is one more type of respirator, most associate with firefighters, the *Self-Contained Breathing Apparatus (SCBA).* These have their own tank air supply so their is no need for filters.

There are color coding for gas mask chemical cartridges/canisters. The color designates the type of contaminant that they filter. Here is a list of some of them you are most likely to use.

Acid gases	All White
Chlorine gas	White with 1/2 inch yellow stripe
Ammonia	Green
Acid and Ammonia	Green with 1/2 inch white stripe
Organic vapors	Black
Pesticides	Organic Black plus a particulate filter
Particulates: N95, N99 or N100	Teal
Particulates: P95, P99, R95, R99, R100	Orange
Particulates: P-100	Purple

There are nine classes of particulate filters which are broken down into three series: N, R, and P. Each series (N, R, and P) is available at three efficiency levels: 95%, 99%, and 99.97%. The N series filter is used in environments free of oil mists. The R series filters can be exposed to oil mists, but should only be worn for one work shift. The P filter can be exposed to oil mists for longer than one work shift. A shift is considered eight hours.

For any mask to work correctly it must have a proper seal fit to the wearer's face. There are different varieties for certain conditions of the wearer:

- The shape of the persons face, facial hair, glasses, thickness and height of head hair all can factor into how well or if a mask will seal properly on a wearer's face. For those that have to wear glasses and not contacts, full face masks can have prescription spectacle kits added to the mask.
- It is best if employees can have their own mask so that it can best fit their own personal requirements. But if not, all

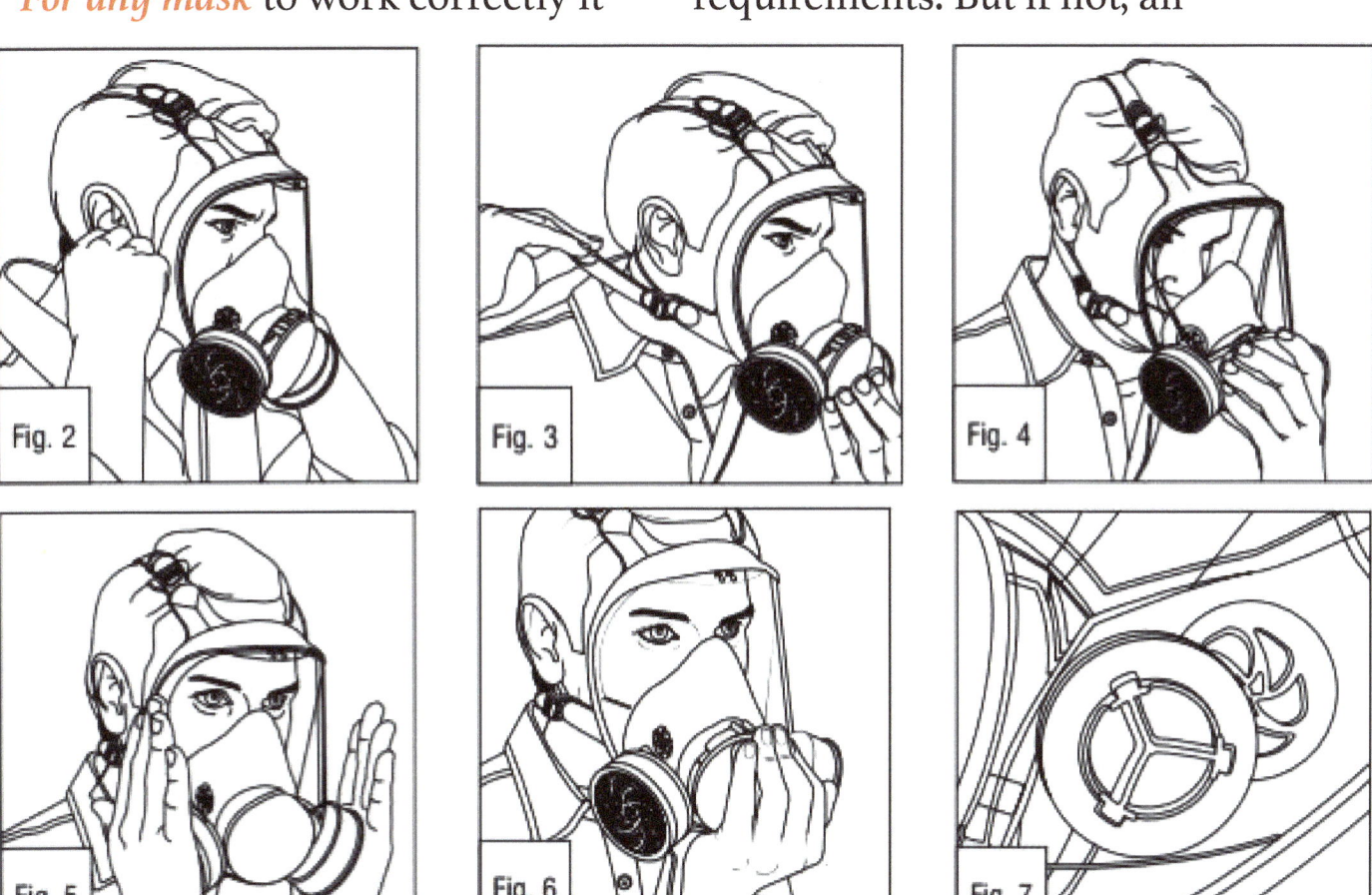

employees need to know how to don, doff, and adjust a mask to the proper fit every time they wear one. This will included the quick suck in and hold your g breath and pull test. If you create a negative pressure inside the mask but can still easily pull it away from your face it does not fit and cannot protect you.

Not everyone can wear a non-air assisted respirator. People with asthma, lung diseases like COPD, emphysema or any reason to have trouble breathing may not be able to move enough air in and out of the mask to use it safely.

RPE will not help you in low oxygen situations, like in a confined space, in a fire, or when there is poor new air circulation.

Donning and Doffing PPE

Every employee that is required to wear any PPE needs to be trained in the correct steps including inspecting, donning, adjusting, doffing, cleaning and storing of the PPE.

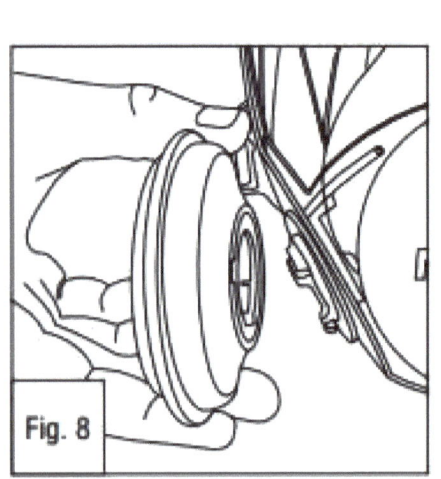
Fig. 8

Per OSHA requirements:

"Workers must properly don (put on) required PPE before entering an area with a potential hazard that requires the use of the PPE. Workers may not remove (doff) required PPE before leaving the area of exposure. Personnel required to wear PPE need to be instructed in proper donning and doffing techniques and inspection procedures."

Any employee that will need to wear and use a respirator while working for you must be trained first before any work is done. Be sure you know by reading your SDS's for your chemicals what type of RPE will be needed to be sure everyone will be properly trained.

About the Author

Linda Chambers is the Brand & Sales Manager for Soap Warehouse brand soaps, part of the Georgia Chemical Equipment (GCE) Company. She enjoys writing articles, blogging, and marketing for the company websites ad social media. To learn more, visit www.SoapWarehouse.biz.

October 19-21, Orlando

The Power Washers of North America (PWNA) is excited to announce that they will be co-locating with CETA (the Cleaning Equipment Trade Association) for a joint trade show at this year's annual PWNA Convention, October 19-21, in Orlando, Fla.

PWNA is the longest-standing trade association for pressure washing industry contractors, while CETA is the premier trade organization for pressure washing manufacturers, distributors and supplier.

The two trade associations coming together for PowerClean 2018 will bring incredible opportunities for attendees – with more exhibitors, equipment training, seminars, networking, and fun.

As the CETA website explains:

"While both associations will remain independent and have events of their own, CETA and the PWNA feel that these two great associations can combine efforts to work towards a common goal. Two teams. One Vision. Advancing the industry forward.

The event will take place at the Caribe Royale, the Orlando area's largest all-suite convention hotel featuring a wealth of amenities. Rooms can be reserved now at a special rate using the special PWNA link.

Watch for more additional details – including the schedule and costs – in upcoming issues of eClean Magazine, as well as on the PWNA Friends and Members Facebook group. To learn more, visit www.PWNA.org or email support@PWNA.org.

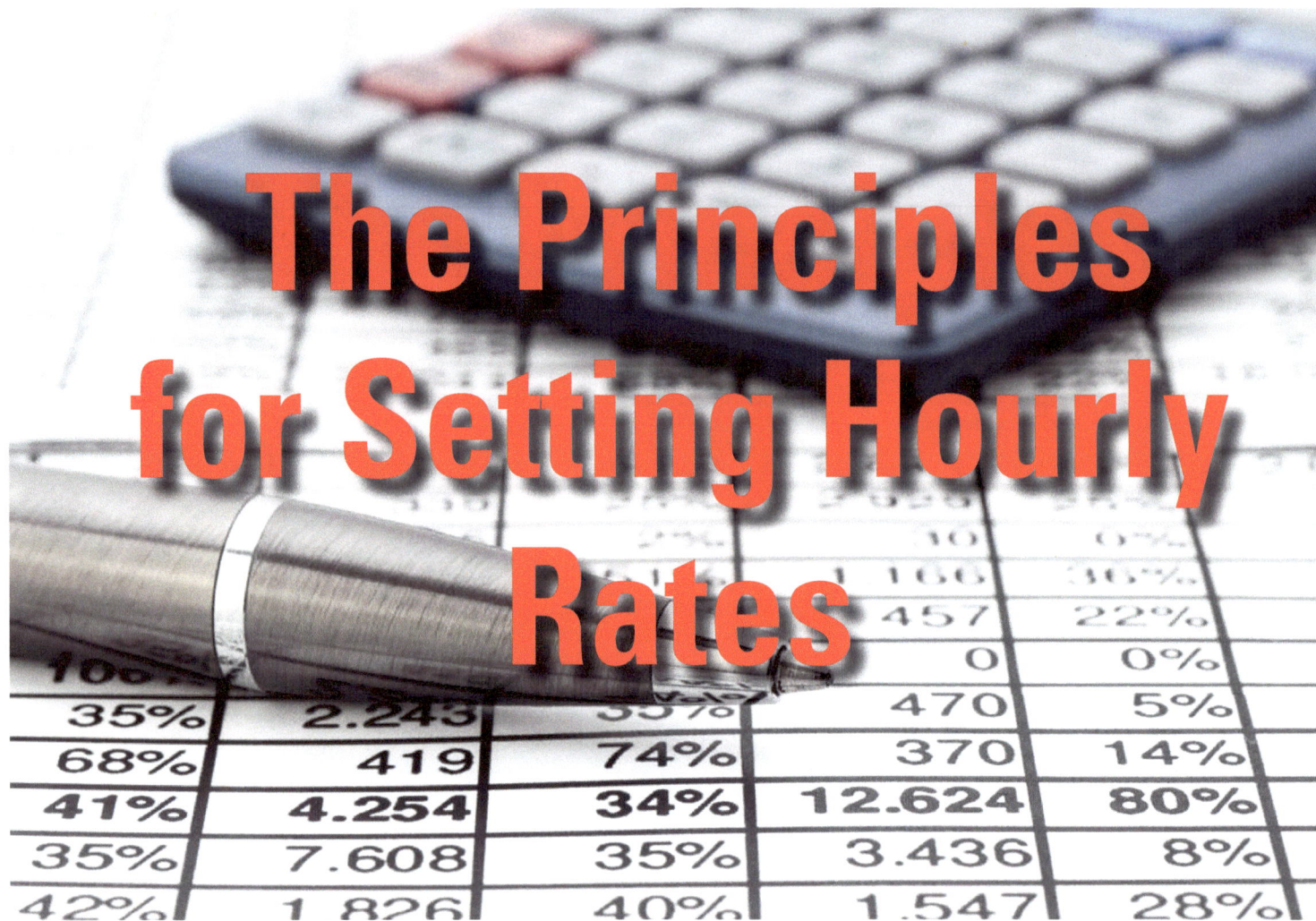

The Principles for Setting Hourly Rates

by Tom Grandy, Grandy & Associates

The foundational principle of proper labor pricing is that rates need to be calculated from a cash-flow perspective, not accounting. Cash flow deals with the *real* dollars that flow in and out of the company verses accounting numbers that sometimes use paper dollars. We will discuss some of the major differences throughout is article.

Equipment Replacement Dollars
There is a major difference between cash flow and accounting. When a vehicle or piece of equipment is purchased, Uncle Sam typically allows the owner to write the cost off over five years, or 20% a year. This becomes a cost of doing business in the form of an overhead cost called depreciation.

Equipment replacement, however, looks at the same piece of equipment from an entirely different point of view. Equipment replacement asks how many more years will the equipment last and what will it cost in the future to replace it, then builds the "future cost" into today's pricing so when it's time to replace the equipment the owner has the cash to pay for it.

Example:

A vehicle was purchased three years ago for $25,000. It is estimated to last four more years and the cost of replacement will be a net $28,000 after trade-in. That means the equipment replace cost would be $7,000 per year ($28,000/4 years = $7,000/year)

Typically, equipment replacement cost will be at least twice the accounting depreciation figure (since it is dealing with past costs, not future costs) and equipment replacement cost will again typically be the company's second highest single cost of doing business.

Labor, Direct and Indirect

Indirect labor covers overhead staff – normally office staff and/or owners, who do not work in the field.

Direct labor covers technicians that are working in the field whose time is normally billed directly to the customer. Direct labor has significant amounts of non-billable time. Non-billable time is composed of shop time at the beginning and end of the day. It also includes travel time between jobs, vacation, sick and holidays, as well as callbacks, warranty work, and company meetings. A typical technician (making multiple calls a day) may have non-billable time in the range of around 20%.

Think about that for a moment. If you have a tech making $18/hour, or perhaps $20/hour when you include company matching taxes, that single tech is costing the company $20,000 a year (1,000 non-billable hours per year X $20/hour = $20,000/year) in non-billable time. That $20,000 needs to become part of the company's overhead cost just like rent, utilities, insurance, etc.

Fixed and Variable Overhead

These are the basic costs of doing business, including gas, insurance, office supplies, etc. However, when listing overhead costs, be sure to include the following overhead costs that are

Amazingly, many company owners do not pay themselves a regular salary; they simply take money out when needed. Well guess what, if you don't build rent, utilities, insurance, etc. into your customer pricing, it won't get covered. Likewise, if you don't build your salary into your cost of doing business, it won't get covered either.

often overlooked.

- Bad debt - Money that is not and will not be collected.
- Debt - Many companies have a lot of past debt that needs to be paid off. This could take the form of past taxes, money owed a supplier, line of credit, personal loans, etc. Decide how many years you want to take to pay off the debt and build the repayment cost into the overhead.
- FULL amount of the loan payment - This is a huge difference in cash flow and accounting. If you have a $500/month loan payment where $100 of it is interest and the other $400 is principle, the only thing that shows up in the accounting P/L statement is the $100 interest. However, from a cash flow perspective, the company wrote a check for $500, which flowed out of the company. If a company has a lot of loans, this can be a major reason your accountant tells you that you are making money (which you will have to pay taxes on) while there is no money in your checkbook!

Material and Equipment Costs

Most of the time when the company purchases materials or equipment to resell to the customer they will mark up the item to generate a net profit. The markup on the items sold can, and will, absorb some of the fixed and variable overhead of running the business.

Owner's Salary

Amazingly, many company owners do not pay themselves a regular salary; they simply take money out when needed. Well guess what, if you don't build rent, utilities, insurance, etc. into your customer pricing, it won't get covered. Likewise, if you don't build your salary into your cost of doing business, it won't get covered either. Put a family budget together to determine what salary you need to earn and build it into your cost of doing business as indirect labor.

We have covered the basic costs of doing business from a cash flow perspective. Now let's look at the simplified steps of setting profitable hourly rates:

Step 1: Calculate the company's total annual Equipment Replacement Costs by listing all vehicles and equipment over $1,000 in value. This will become one of your fixed overhead costs a bit later.

Step 2: Total all indirect labor cost and be sure to include your costs of matching taxes (matching Social Security, Federal Unemployment Tax, and your unique State Unemployment Rate.)

Step 3: Do three things when it comes to direct labor in the field.
1. Determine the cost of non-billable time which will become

an overhead cost.

2. Determine the actual number of billable hours to the customer (total hours the company pays for, less non-billable hours).

3. Determine the weighted average hourly rate of all direct labor personnel

Step 4: Total the real cost of doing business including fixed and variable overhead, direct and indirect labor, cost of non-billable time, full amount of loan payments, equipment replacement costs and matching taxes.

Step 5: Project how much gross profit will be generated through the sale of materials and equipment over the coming year.

Step 6: Calculate the overhead rate per hour. Take the total cost of doing business calculated in Step 4 and subtract the projected gross profit calculated in Step 5 then divide the remaining number by the BILLABLE hours determined in Step 3.

For our example's sake, your overhead rate is $48.78/hour.

Step 7: Determine the break-even hourly rate. This is the rate you would need to cover all the companies' costs of doing business but would NOT generate a net profit. The break-even rate is the combination of the overhead rate per hour in Step 6, which was $48.78/hour, and the average hourly rate of the direct labor people. If the average rate were perhaps $16.53, the break-even rate would be $65.31.

Step 8: The final rate is determined by adding profit to the equation. If we wanted to generate a 10% net profit we would divide the break-even rate by .9. Let's assume the company wants a 15% net profit. The needed hourly rate would then be:

= $65.31 / $.85
= $76.83/hour

In its simplest form, that is the process. If you need a bit of help check out our website at www.GrandyAssociates.com/LP

www.ingramcontent.com/pod-product-compliance
Lightning Source LLC
Chambersburg PA
CBHW040453220526
45473CB00004B/1618